Scarlet Shadows

© 2019 Scylla Grand
All rights reserved.
ISBN: 978-1-7340429-0-0

Scarlet is the color I see
when my eyes are *closed*
and I am swathed in sunlight.

Acknowledgments

CJ, Tori, Tiana, Amber, Ross, Jen, Lillian, Grace,
thank you for supporting my poetic endeavors.

Table of Contents

I. Invisible
  1. "Red Leaf"
  2. "Monsters"
  3. "Wine and Bread"
  4. "Black Diamond"
  5. "Loving Starts"
  6. "Vanishing Ground"
  7. "Betrayal Is"
  8. "Fury"
  9. "Muted Sound"

II. Inertia
  10. "Unoccupied"
  11. "Snowfall"
  12. "Sirens"
  13. "Ignorance"
  14. "Planes"
  15. "Icing"
  16. "None"
  17. "Hush"
  18. "Reciprocation"
  19. "Rice and Tea"
  20. "A Figure"
  21. "Reverie"

III. Cold
  22. "Lethal"
  23. "Dust"
  24. "Webs and Blooms"
  25. "Sea and Ocean"
  26. "Unfortunately"
  27. "Into My Shell"
  28. "Snow Is Falling"
  29. "On Living Coals"
  30. "Beast"

I. Invisible

"Red Leaf"

no one paints the red leaf wilting,
steeped in mud disturbed by boots.
none observe its slow decay;
it sleeps in paint a perfect hue.

"Monsters"

The monsters parading know me as kin;
I march in their skin
but want to escape.
I hide in the bathroom, claiming I'm sick.
Surrounded by walls, I think I am safe.

I shudder and rip
the skin off my flesh -
illusory mesh
decided by script.
It's me in the mirror, free and unkempt.

A knock on the door; they know I exist.
I quickly prepare a game of pretend.
Discarding my id,
I grow and mature
as all of my skin encloses again.

The horrors I see, I am. What endures
past childhood hides
like hope in the jar
surrounded by monsters, locked in the heart.

"Wine and Bread"

the woman fed us wine and bread
and hungry, I should eat my fill
but food so fine could not be mine
I ate, but I was starving still

"Black Diamond"

the blackest diamond of them all -
so well-concealed, it can't be found -
cannot be parted from the heart,
cannot be raised from underground.

you tell me I am beautiful;
I listen, but I don't believe.
my morbid thoughts absorb what light
my spirit wishes to receive.

the truth embedded in my heart -
that wretched diamond - cannot crack.
it tells me I'm invisible;
it wraps me in a peerless black.

"Loving Starts"

The tiny batch
of glowing matches
quivers as the child catches
cold despite the warming light.

The matches die;
she quickly tires
with the dying of the fires...
still alive as friends arrive.

Though all that's bright
is fire, rightly,
not all fires can burn brightly,
nor all hearts have loving starts.

"Vanishing Ground"

Ground ahead is vanishing.
I'm counting sand again, again:
thirty pebbles on my palm.
Vanished all but thirty then.

What provisions do I bring
Tomorrow, to restrain the blight
of nausea rising easily?
Gone the flame, so gone the light.

Thirty matches yet to fade -
brighter now that darkness lands -
warm the candle, brave the wind,
and pave anew a path of sand.

"Betrayal Is"

Betrayal is a fruitless seed
that cannot grow and may not leave.
But I don't mind her company.

She's not her mother, nor is she
a badge of how her mother won
and scraped the insight off my tongue,

and chipped my teeth, and cut my lip.
I see myself, a lurching lich
of charcoal black and vulgar ridges,
stretched and bent.

How beautiful, betrayal shows
upon my face.
And in her mother's place, I hold
Betrayal's hand until she goes.

"Fury"

My fury is a sterile white -

a sky of constellations lost
in melding with the morning light.

A million vivid hues exhaust
my eyes, but still my vision thrives.
In darkness, I saw nothing wrong.
In daytime, now - the truth arrives.

The words you murmured crawl along
my palm. In bliss, I watch them die.

I feel malicious, mad delight

and laugh, as neither you nor I
will miss the blackness of the night.

"Muted Sound"

the muted sound
of tightened rope

is lost but through
a microscope

II. Inertia

"Unoccupied"

I sculpted living, wooden dolls
that splintered in the slicing wind.

I kept a morgue. I could recall
each person laid inside a bin.

At night, the starving winds withdrew.

I picked survivors off the shore
and pieced them whole

again.
Monsoons
would pull them back, deceased and torn.

The last collapsed.
I closed my mind,
my heart a boundless vacancy.

A darkened room,
a window,
light.
But I could not see anything.

Directionless, I searched the morgue -
a massive grid of ruptured safes
where nothing lingered anymore...

What reason did I have to stay?

The longest silence stretched.
I slowed,

then saw one speck,
a teasing flame

of colors
I had yet to know

and pieces I had yet to place.

"Snowfall"

Snow was softly falling, light
as powder bursting. I
stared into the endless crowd
of captivating white.
Once a snowflake met my face,
it melted. Arctic shade
could not touch me. Paradise:
I knew at last the place.

"Sirens"

The tranquil sea, opaque at night,
entices humans to the shore
where sirens perch like harpy-kind,
beseeching those they once adored,
awaiting – watching – side by side.

At every death, a shadow forms,
a phantom still embracing life,
its body – smoke, like breathing coals;
its core – a scorching molten-white;
the markings of a siren born.

It wanders over solemn waves,
impelled by worldly memories,
toward the effervescent flames
that gather on the starving beach,
as if they called it out to play.

The sirens burn with mellow heat,
a soothing warmth that never fades.
To hear them is to rest in peace.
Like will-o-wisps, they light the way,
a beacon far beyond the sea.

"Ignorance"

knowing: unknowingness pulls me aside
favors the strongest, yet I with my pride
staunch my direction by closing my eyes
holding, beholding, my glorified prize
deep in my mind, undefeatable I
swoop through the air on a meaningless high
how many cycles of time slip away
walking, just walking, with nowhere to stay
searching for pardon, a promise, an aid
all to extend my pathetic parade
yet, I recall, through those fragmented years
ignorance sheltered me, canceled my fears
raised my morale, and cemented me whole
brought me the marbles reality stole

"Planes"

The people dance on floors of stone.
They never stop nor blink, despite
my being helplessly alone.
They glide like airplanes stuck in flight:
a world that functions on its own.
And I, a distant oversight,

think maybe planes can't turn around
to entertain a second glance
at those who watch them from the ground.
The song compels them all to dance;
I move toward the lilting sound -
and lose them in the dark expanse.

The shadows swallow up the street,
the song a wistful lullaby.
I dance alone, a bittersweet
pursuit. Without discerning why,
I falter for a single beat
to watch the murky, muted sky.

I sometimes wonder, could it be -
that plane forever passing through
the evening's airy filigree
has lost me in the darkness too;
and there is someone missing me
as much as I am missing you.

"Icing"

I licked the icing off the cake
surrendered to its creamy taste
but once I blinked, the magic faded
spoiled by an absent weight

"None"

I'd like to find a partner to
embrace forever in my heart;
to journey with, for company;
to raise me up when life's too hard.

I found a few I almost loved
but felt the fit was always off.
I cared in ways they never did;
they cared in ways that I did not.

The ones I loved - I let them fly;
restraint serves no one in the end.
But every person that I loved
I freed - and never saw again.

I searched for one as lost as me -
my missing pieces filled by theirs -
but where I looked I could not find
my perfect likeness anywhere.

"Hush"

In moonlit nights, an earnest sigh
arouses pensive, fretful sleep
like apathetic paws that lure
then grasp your mind without a peep

The aspirations for today
those fruitless gems - untouched, unsown
which kept your spirit ironclad
are ceaseless in their steady glow

As sunshine steals away, the day
disperses into nighttime hush
Despite another waste or gain
unsatisfied abides the crush

"Reciprocation"

A wing descends, creates a gust,
then reaches upward, as it must,
to strike the air again, to rise.
I envy birds those endless skies.

I lifted spirits, raised them high.
I loved without a reason why
but searched for echoes nonetheless
and heard unbroken quietness.

With tired voice and jaded mind,
I left the battlefront resigned.
Exhausted eagles do not fly;
they cannot lift their wings - they die.

"Rice and Tea"

Inside the burning cup of tea,
a grain of rice begins to sink.
I slide a piece of ice beneath -
a single floatie in the sea -
and smile to myself, relieved,
like someone kind had rescued me.

"A Figure"

I fear my touch will mar his face,
contort his limb as in a brace.
Already bones are misaligning,
yet I must not look away.

I carve my symbol into paper,
twist my hand to fit his shape.
A focused stare, invoking life,
creates a vision on the page.

"Reverie"

At tower's peak, I find myself,
adrift in reverie –
Although I fear abysmal heights,
to heights I often flee.

A deep and vacant pool – the sky
surrounds the tiny me.
Those puzzle pieces called the Earth
are gently pulling free.
I'm sliding, I am scattering
above a drop so steep –

My wayward thoughts consolidate
like whiplash, once I leap.

It's not so strange, I think, to dream
of places of allure.
If fear is our shared disease,
then motive is the cure.

III. Cold

"Lethal"

Our team became forbidden wings:
a crude construction challenging
the lofty sun, the summer sky;
a flock of feathers matched in might;
a codex held together, bound
by rivalry, like sky and ground.

We glided in the orange heat
in practiced choreography.
Like Icarus, we climbed the sky
and touched it at its noble height.
We knew no better feat than this:
to make the golden sun eclipsed.

But at the peak our bond collapsed;
we scattered free, as melted wax
relieved us of our source of pride.
We shone like blades of lethal ice,
an avalanche of ceaseless dreams
cascading down to meet the sea.

"Dust"

The dust collects
  upon my skin
    by hailing stone,
      adhering, draping
        cuts. Infection
          slits my bone.

I rise to dust
  inspection off.
    My legs unlock.
      The drape cascading
        unattaches
          as I walk.

"Webs and Blooms"

From the corners spiders crept,
slinking, small, and leaking lead,
stretched across and overhead.
The more I lost, the more they fed.

I heard their footsteps spelling doom
to me and all within the room.
I found a pot of ink to use;
then I drew a little bloom.

I placed the bloom beside the webs
and looked to hope as much as dread.
Although the nesting spiders spread,
bit by bit discomfort fled.

On the wall, that flower bloomed,
subduing pain with sweet perfume.
I scattered fragrance to the moon
and with the growing flowers grew.

"Sea and Ocean"

I see an island, dreaming
I am carried by the sea,
which laps around me, spinning
waves of wind on every leaf.
The ocean - far but coming -
wraps its arms around my knees.
I dream no longer, seeing
wishes sinking, out of reach.

Imprisonment is final.
Am I doomed to flounder, blind?
I've lost the path to surface,
swim, in absence of my sight;
but movements - recollected -
sit inside me, warm and dry.
I've countless little islands,
reaching out toward the skies.

"Unfortunately"

you're cold and rude - I know you are -
but still I linger on the stair
I listen for your voice from far
beyond your reach, beyond your care

your laughter - or your tear-stained eyes -
can prod my heart to life again
I know your name, but nothing ties
me now to you, as tied us then

in desperate times, I think of you -
a soothing and remorseful thought
I hate you, but you see me through
no matter if you're here or not

"Into My Shell"

lightning never ends
my reservoir descends
below the line, my mind declines
to depths without amends

instead of interacting
sometimes I retract
beneath my skin and stay therein
to keep myself intact

yet someone once would peek
beneath my covers bleak
would lure me out with fruit and sprout
then peck me on the cheek

the world right then was bold
with flavors - bright, untold
although I shook, I'd overlook
the lightning, ever gold

"Snow Is Falling"

the snow is ever falling, falling
sliding to the ground
how could a foe be lurking, lurking
here without a sound?

the summer's drought consumed my tears
without a pause to rest
instead of crying, warm and dry
to never hurt is best

the fall of snow is soothing, soothing
nothing scares me now
just watch the snowfall building, building
high as skies allow

the sting of heat has grown so weak
my burns have healed at last
I shouldn't - but already seek
the light through overcast

my mother tells me, shushing, shushing
cloaks the sun from view
just watch the nothing falling, falling
calmly into you

"On Living Coals"

I trudged across a lake of flame,
dismissed the screaming of my soles,
and stifled every nerve, to claim
my prize beyond those living coals.

An eon passed. At last, I found
resplendent gems inside a cup
embedded in a snowy ground.
Without a pause, I snatched them up.

My pain had vanished with the heat;
with joy, I thought I must have healed,
until I noticed that my feet
could not detect the chilly field.

That moment, I became aware
that wounds forgotten still are there.

"Beast"

You tuck away the compromised -
that memory you once had prized,
when at a touch, mirth's brilliant gloss
is blemished by a sour loss.
But banished thoughts despite your will
are breathing and surviving still.

The moment stalks your mind unbowed;
its roar contaminates the crowd.
Regarding it with care and fright,
you tell yourself, "Don't let it bite."
You tread toward the center stage
and lure the beast into a cage.

Before it fades, remember this:
When winter storms extinguished bliss,
the beast had kindled warmth in you.
And this forever will be true.
Your moment thwarts the parasite
called ice with its surpassing might.

Survival is a fickle trail
of endless storms and sudden hail.
Release the creature locked inside -
that tainted soul you once denied.
And when you free the beast, behold!
It follows you into the cold.

www.ingramcontent.com/pod-product-compliance
Lightning Source LLC
Chambersburg PA
CBHW021639080526
44584CB00015BA/1600